EMMANUEL JOSEPH

The Art of Inner Peace: Crafting a Calm Mind in a Chaotic World

Copyright © 2025 by Emmanuel Joseph

All rights reserved. No part of this publication may be reproduced, stored or transmitted in any form or by any means, electronic, mechanical, photocopying, recording, scanning, or otherwise without written permission from the publisher. It is illegal to copy this book, post it to a website, or distribute it by any other means without permission.

First edition

This book was professionally typeset on Reedsy. Find out more at reedsy.com

Contents

1	Chapter 1: Understanding Inner Peace	1
2	Chapter 2: The Mind-Body Connection	3
3	Chapter 3: Managing Stress and Anxiety	5
4	Chapter 4: Embracing Mindfulness	7
5	Chapter 5: The Power of Positive Thinking	9
6	Chapter 6: Building Resilience	11
7	Chapter 7: Nurturing Self-Compassion	13
8	Chapter 8: Cultivating Gratitude	15
9	Chapter 9: Finding Balance in Life	17
10	Chapter 10: The Role of Relationships	19
11	Chapter 11: The Journey of Personal Growth	21
12	Chapter 12: Sustaining Inner Peace	23

1

Chapter 1: Understanding Inner Peace

Inner peace is the cornerstone of a balanced life. It involves a deep sense of harmony and tranquility that originates within. Unlike fleeting happiness, inner peace is enduring and resilient, allowing individuals to navigate life's storms with equanimity. By cultivating self-awareness and acceptance, one can begin the journey toward achieving this profound state of calm.

Developing inner peace requires introspection and self-compassion. It is essential to recognize and embrace one's imperfections and vulnerabilities. This process fosters a sense of self-love and understanding, which are crucial for inner tranquility. By letting go of self-judgment and external validation, one can find solace within.

Mindfulness plays a pivotal role in nurturing inner peace. It involves being fully present in the moment, observing thoughts and feelings without judgment. This practice helps individuals detach from negative thought patterns and emotional turbulence, paving the way for mental clarity and serenity. Regular mindfulness practice can transform the mind into a sanctuary of peace.

Inner peace is not a destination but a continuous journey. It requires consistent effort and dedication. By integrating mindfulness, self-compassion, and self-awareness into daily life, individuals can cultivate a lasting sense of peace. This chapter sets the foundation for exploring the various facets of inner peace in the subsequent chapters.

2

Chapter 2: The Mind-Body Connection

The mind and body are inextricably linked, each influencing the other in profound ways. A calm mind promotes physical well-being, while a healthy body supports mental tranquility. Understanding this connection is vital for achieving holistic health and inner peace. This chapter explores the interplay between the mind and body and offers practical exercises to harmonize the two.

Physical health significantly impacts mental well-being. Regular exercise, a balanced diet, and adequate sleep are essential for maintaining a healthy body. These practices not only enhance physical health but also elevate mood, reduce stress, and boost mental clarity. By prioritizing physical well-being, individuals can create a solid foundation for inner peace.

Mindfulness and meditation are powerful tools for bridging the mind-body gap. These practices cultivate a deep awareness of bodily sensations, thoughts, and emotions. By tuning into the present moment, individuals can release physical tension and mental stress. This chapter provides guided exercises to help readers integrate mindfulness and meditation into their daily routines.

The mind-body connection also involves acknowledging and addressing emotional pain. Unresolved emotions can manifest as physical ailments, and vice versa. By exploring and healing emotional wounds, individuals can achieve a state of holistic well-being. This chapter offers insights into emotional healing techniques, promoting a harmonious mind-body relationship.

3

Chapter 3: Managing Stress and Anxiety

Stress and anxiety are pervasive in today's fast-paced world. However, with the right tools and mindset, these conditions can be managed effectively. This chapter provides a comprehensive guide to understanding and alleviating stress and anxiety, empowering readers to regain control over their mental well-being.

Recognizing the sources of stress is the first step toward managing it. Stress can stem from various aspects of life, including work, relationships, and personal expectations. By identifying stressors, individuals can develop strategies to mitigate their impact. This chapter encourages readers to engage in self-reflection to pinpoint their unique stress triggers.

Various techniques can help manage stress and anxiety. Deep breathing exercises, progressive muscle relaxation, and mindfulness meditation are proven methods for reducing stress. These practices activate the body's relaxation response, counteracting the physiological effects of stress. This chapter provides step-by-step instructions for implementing these techniques.

Cognitive restructuring is another effective tool for managing anxiety. It involves challenging and reframing negative thought patterns that contribute to anxiety. By adopting a more positive and realistic perspective, individuals can reduce their anxiety levels. This chapter offers practical tips for cognitive restructuring, helping readers cultivate a more balanced mindset.

Incorporating self-care into daily life is crucial for managing stress and anxiety. Activities such as journaling, spending time in nature, and engaging in hobbies can provide a sense of relaxation and fulfillment. This chapter emphasizes the importance of self-care and encourages readers to prioritize their well-being.

11

Chapter 11: The Journey of Personal Growth

Personal growth is an ongoing journey of self-discovery and improvement. It's about setting goals, embracing challenges, and continuously evolving. This chapter encourages readers to embark on their journey of personal growth, providing tools and inspiration for self-improvement.

Personal growth begins with self-awareness. It involves understanding one's strengths, weaknesses, and areas for improvement. By engaging in self-reflection, individuals can identify their goals and aspirations, paving the way for personal development. This chapter provides guidance on self-assessment and goal-setting.

Embracing challenges is a crucial aspect of personal growth. By stepping out of our comfort zones and facing difficulties head-on, we can develop resilience and learn valuable lessons. This chapter encourages readers to view challenges as opportunities for growth and offers strategies for overcoming obstacles.

Continuous learning is essential for personal growth. It involves seeking out new experiences, acquiring knowledge, and developing skills. This chapter emphasizes the importance of lifelong learning and provides tips for staying curious and motivated on the journey of self-improvement.

Personal growth also involves self-compassion and self-care. It is essential to nurture oneself and practice self-kindness throughout the journey. This chapter encourages readers to prioritize their well-being and offers practical advice for integrating self-compassion into their personal growth endeavors.

12

Chapter 12: Sustaining Inner Peace

Achieving inner peace is a continuous process that requires ongoing effort and commitment. This final chapter offers strategies for sustaining inner peace over the long term, including maintaining healthy habits, seeking support when needed, and staying connected to one's inner self.

Maintaining inner peace involves integrating healthy habits into daily life. Practices such as mindfulness, gratitude, and self-care should be consistently upheld to preserve a sense of tranquility. This chapter provides practical tips for sustaining these habits and making them a part of daily routines.

Seeking support from others is also crucial for sustaining inner peace. Building a network of supportive friends, family, and mentors can provide encouragement and guidance during challenging times. This chapter emphasizes the importance of seeking and offering support within relationships, fostering a sense of community and resilience.

Staying connected to one's inner self is essential for sustaining inner peace. Regular self-reflection, meditation, and mindfulness practices can help individuals maintain a deep sense of self-awareness and tranquility. This chapter encourages readers to cultivate a strong connection with their inner selves and offers practical exercises for self-exploration.

Inner peace is a lifelong journey. It requires dedication, patience, and a commitment to personal growth. By embracing the practices and principles discussed in this book, individuals can craft a calm mind and navigate the chaotic world with grace and resilience. This final chapter serves as a reminder that inner peace is attainable and worth striving for.

Book Description: The Art of Inner Peace: Crafting a Calm Mind in a Chaotic World

In the frenetic pace of today's world, finding inner peace can seem like an elusive dream. However, "The Art of Inner Peace: Crafting a Calm Mind in a Chaotic World" offers a comprehensive guide to achieving tranquility amidst the chaos. This book delves into the essential elements of inner peace, presenting practical techniques and profound insights to help readers cultivate a serene and balanced life.

Across twelve enlightening chapters, the author explores various aspects of inner peace, from understanding the foundational principles to implementing effective stress management strategies. The book emphasizes the interconnectedness of mind and body, illustrating how practices like mindfulness, meditation, and positive thinking can harmonize one's mental and physical well-being.

Readers will find valuable advice on building resilience, nurturing self-compassion, and fostering gratitude. Each chapter provides practical exercises and actionable steps, encouraging readers to integrate these practices into their daily lives. With a focus on holistic well-being, the book also highlights the importance of maintaining healthy relationships and finding balance in all areas of life.

"The Art of Inner Peace" is more than just a guide—it's a journey of self-discovery and personal growth. It invites readers to embark on a transformative path toward lasting inner tranquility, equipping them with the tools to navigate life's challenges with grace and resilience. Whether you are new to the concept of inner peace or seeking to deepen your practice, this book is a valuable companion on your quest for a calm and harmonious mind.

www.ingramcontent.com/pod-product-compliance
Lightning Source LLC
LaVergne TN
LVHW010445070526
838199LV00066B/6204

The Art of Inner Peace: Crafting a Calm Mind in a Chaotic World In the frenetic pace of today's world, finding inner peace can seem like an elusive dream. However, "The Art of Inner Peace: Crafting a Calm Mind in a Chaotic World" offers a comprehensive guide to achieving tranquility amidst the chaos. This book delves into the essential elements of inner peace, presenting practical techniques and profound insights to help readers cultivate a serene and balanced life. Across twelve enlightening chapters, the author explores various aspects of inner peace, from understanding the foundational principles to implementing effective stress management strategies. The book emphasizes the interconnectedness of mind and body, illustrating how practices like mindfulness, meditation, and positive thinking can harmonize one's mental and physical well-being. Readers will find valuable advice on building resilience, nurturing self-compassion, and fostering gratitude. Each chapter provides practical exercises and actionable steps, encouraging readers to integrate these practices into their daily lives. With a focus on holistic well-being, the book also highlights the importance of maintaining healthy relationships and finding balance in all areas of life. "The Art of Inner Peace" is more than just a guide—it's a journey of self-discovery and personal growth. It invites readers to embark on a transformative path toward lasting inner tranquility, equipping them with the tools to navigate life's challenges with grace and resilience. Whether you are new to the concept of inner peace or seeking to deepen your practice, this book is a valuable companion on your quest for a calm and harmonious mind.

4

Chapter 4: Embracing Mindfulness

Mindfulness is the practice of being fully present in the moment, without judgment. It allows individuals to experience life with greater clarity and depth. By cultivating mindfulness, one can reduce stress, enhance focus, and improve emotional resilience. This chapter explores the principles of mindfulness and offers practical tips for integrating it into daily life.

The essence of mindfulness lies in non-judgmental awareness. It involves observing thoughts, emotions, and sensations without labeling them as good or bad. This practice helps individuals detach from negative thought patterns and emotional reactions, promoting mental clarity and tranquility. This chapter introduces readers to the foundational concepts of mindfulness.

Mindfulness can be practiced in various forms, including meditation, mindful breathing, and mindful movement. These practices encourage individuals to anchor their awareness in the present moment, fostering a sense of calm and focus. This chapter provides guided exercises for different mindfulness practices, making it accessible for beginners and seasoned practitioners alike.

Incorporating mindfulness into daily life requires consistency and dedication. Simple activities such as mindful eating, walking, and listening can transform mundane moments into opportunities for mindfulness. This chapter offers practical tips for integrating mindfulness into everyday routines, helping readers cultivate a mindful lifestyle.

Mindfulness also involves cultivating an attitude of curiosity and openness. By approaching experiences with a beginner's mind, individuals can fully engage with the present moment and appreciate its richness. This chapter encourages readers to adopt a curious and open-minded approach to life, enhancing their mindfulness practice.

5

Chapter 5: The Power of Positive Thinking

Positive thinking is a powerful tool for transforming one's outlook on life. It involves focusing on the good in every situation and maintaining an optimistic mindset. By cultivating positive thoughts, individuals can enhance their mental well-being and resilience. This chapter examines the impact of positive thinking and offers strategies for developing a positive mindset.

Our thoughts shape our reality. Positive thinking can influence how we perceive and react to the world around us. It promotes a sense of optimism and hope, which are crucial for mental health. This chapter explores the science behind positive thinking and its effects on the brain and overall well-being.

Developing a positive mindset requires conscious effort and practice. Techniques such as affirmations, visualization, and gratitude exercises can help individuals cultivate positive thoughts. By consistently focusing on positive aspects of life, one can gradually shift their mindset. This chapter provides practical exercises for fostering positive thinking.

Positive thinking does not mean ignoring challenges or denying negative emotions. It involves acknowledging difficulties while choosing to focus on solutions and opportunities. This balanced approach allows individuals to navigate life's ups and downs with resilience. This chapter emphasizes the importance of maintaining a realistic yet optimistic perspective.

Positive thinking also involves surrounding oneself with positive influences. Supportive relationships, inspirational books, and uplifting environments can reinforce a positive mindset. This chapter encourages readers to seek out positive influences and create a supportive network, enhancing their journey toward positive thinking.

6

Chapter 6: Building Resilience

Resilience is the ability to bounce back from setbacks and thrive despite challenges. It is a crucial component of inner peace, enabling individuals to navigate life's ups and downs with grace. This chapter delves into the characteristics of resilient individuals and provides practical advice for building resilience.

Resilience is rooted in a positive mindset and a sense of purpose. It involves viewing challenges as opportunities for growth and learning. By adopting a growth mindset, individuals can develop resilience and approach difficulties with confidence. This chapter explores the principles of resilience and how to cultivate a resilient mindset.

Building resilience requires developing coping strategies for dealing with stress and adversity. Techniques such as problem-solving, emotional regulation, and social support can enhance resilience. This chapter offers practical tips for implementing these strategies, helping readers strengthen their resilience.

Resilience also involves self-care and self-compassion. Taking care of one's physical, emotional, and mental well-being is essential for maintaining resilience. This chapter emphasizes the importance of self-care practices, such as exercise, relaxation, and seeking support, in building resilience.

Resilient individuals possess a strong support network. Building and maintaining healthy relationships can provide a sense of belonging and emotional support. This chapter discusses the role of social connections in resilience and offers advice for nurturing positive relationships.

7

Chapter 7: Nurturing Self-Compassion

Self-compassion involves treating oneself with kindness and understanding, especially during difficult times. It is an essential aspect of inner peace, fostering self-acceptance and emotional healing. This chapter explores the concept of self-compassion and provides exercises for nurturing a compassionate relationship with oneself.

Self-compassion is about recognizing one's humanity and imperfections. It involves acknowledging that everyone experiences struggles and setbacks. By embracing one's vulnerabilities, individuals can cultivate self-compassion. This chapter encourages readers to practice self-acceptance and let go of self-judgment.

Self-compassion also involves self-care and self-kindness. Taking time to nurture oneself and engage in activities that bring joy and relaxation is crucial for emotional well-being. This chapter offers practical tips for incorporating self-care into daily life, promoting self-compassion.

Mindfulness plays a significant role in self-compassion. By observing one's thoughts and emotions without judgment, individuals can develop a deeper understanding of their inner experiences. This practice fosters self-compassion by creating space for self-reflection and self-awareness. This chapter provides guided mindfulness exercises for cultivating self-compassion.

Building self-compassion requires challenging negative self-talk and replacing it with positive affirmations. By speaking to oneself with kindness and encouragement, individuals can develop a more compassionate inner dialogue. This chapter offers practical strategies for transforming self-talk and nurturing self-compassion.

8

Chapter 8: Cultivating Gratitude

Gratitude is the practice of recognizing and appreciating the positive aspects of life. It shifts our focus from what we lack to what we have, promoting a Gratitude is the practice of recognizing and appreciating the positive aspects of life. It shifts our focus from what we lack to what we have, promoting a sense of contentment and well-being. This chapter discusses the benefits of gratitude and offers practical tips for cultivating a grateful mindset, enhancing overall happiness.

Practicing gratitude can significantly improve mental and emotional well-being. By regularly acknowledging the good in our lives, we can foster a sense of contentment and joy. This practice helps to shift our focus away from negative thoughts and complaints, allowing us to appreciate the present moment. This chapter explores the various ways in which gratitude can be integrated into daily life.

Gratitude journaling is a powerful tool for cultivating a grateful mindset. By writing down things we are thankful for each day, we can train our minds to recognize and appreciate the positive aspects of life. This chapter provides guidance on starting a gratitude journal and offers prompts to inspire reflection and gratitude.

Cultivating gratitude also involves expressing appreciation to others. By acknowledging the kindness and support of those around us, we can strengthen relationships and foster a sense of connection. This chapter encourages readers to practice acts of gratitude, such as writing thank-you notes or verbally expressing appreciation, and discusses the impact of gratitude on interpersonal relationships.

9

Chapter 9: Finding Balance in Life

Achieving inner peace requires finding balance in all areas of life, including work, relationships, and personal time. It's about setting boundaries, prioritizing self-care, and managing time effectively. This chapter provides a comprehensive guide to finding balance, helping readers create a harmonious and fulfilling life.

Finding balance involves assessing and prioritizing different aspects of life. It is essential to identify what matters most and allocate time and energy accordingly. By setting clear boundaries and priorities, individuals can create a balanced and fulfilling lifestyle. This chapter offers practical tips for evaluating and prioritizing various aspects of life.

Self-care is a crucial component of finding balance. Taking time to nurture oneself and engage in activities that promote well-being is essential for maintaining harmony. This chapter emphasizes the importance of self-care practices, such as relaxation, exercise, and pursuing hobbies, and provides guidance on incorporating self-care into daily routines.

Effective time management is another key aspect of finding balance. By planning and organizing tasks efficiently, individuals can make the most of their time and reduce stress. This chapter provides time management strategies, such as creating schedules, setting goals, and avoiding procrastination, to help readers achieve a balanced lifestyle.

Finding balance also involves fostering healthy relationships. Building and maintaining positive connections with others can provide support and enhance well-being. This chapter discusses the role of relationships in achieving balance and offers advice for nurturing meaningful connections with family, friends, and colleagues.

10

Chapter 10: The Role of Relationships

Healthy relationships are a cornerstone of inner peace. They provide support, love, and a sense of belonging. This chapter explores the importance of nurturing positive relationships and offers advice for building and maintaining healthy connections with others.

Strong relationships are built on trust, communication, and mutual respect. It is essential to cultivate these qualities in our interactions with others to create a supportive and loving environment. This chapter discusses the key components of healthy relationships and provides tips for fostering trust and effective communication.

Maintaining healthy relationships requires effort and commitment. Regularly spending quality time with loved ones, expressing appreciation, and resolving conflicts constructively are crucial for sustaining positive connections. This chapter offers practical advice for maintaining and strengthening relationships, enhancing overall well-being.

Relationships also play a significant role in providing emotional support. During challenging times, the presence of supportive friends and family can make a significant difference. This chapter emphasizes the importance of seeking and offering support within relationships, fostering a sense of community and resilience.

Building new relationships and expanding one's social network can also enhance well-being. Engaging in social activities, joining groups, and reaching out to others can provide opportunities for connection and personal growth. This chapter encourages readers to actively seek out and nurture new relationships, enriching their lives with diverse connections.